300 Crazy UK Facts

Utopia Press

The United Kingdom consists of four different countries. They are England, Scotland, Wales, and Northern Ireland

The capital of England is London.

The official language of the United Kingdom is English

The United Kingdom has a population of over 67.3 million people

---

The United Kingdom has a constitutional monarchy. This means the monarch has
limited powers and their role is mostly ceremonial

Queen Elizabeth II was the longest reigning monarch in the world until her death. She
reigned in the UK for 70 years and 214 days

The current monarch of the United Kingdom is King Charles III. He is head of state of
the United Kingdom and 14 Commonwealth states

Queen Consort Camilla is the second wife of King Charles III. The King remarried in
2005 after his first wife, Princess Diana, whom he had divorced in 1996, died

---

The United Kingdom has a parliamentary system of government, with the Prime Minister as the head of government

The current prime minister of the United Kingdom is Rishi Sunak

The official name of the UK is the United Kingdom of Great Britain and Northern Ireland

The United Kingdom is also known as Great Britain or the UK

Great Britain is the name given to three nations on the main isle. These are England, Scotland and Wales

---

Britain is used to refer to only the mainland countries: England and Wales

---

The United Kingdom is located in north-western Europe

The UK is located mainly on two large islands in the Atlantic Ocean: the islands of Great Britain and Ireland

---

English has been the dominant language in the United Kingdom for over 1,000 years

---

The English language is one of the largest languages in the world with over 170,000 words

The English language has borrowed words from many different languages, including French, Latin, Greek, and German

---

Shakespeare is one of the most famous writers in English language history, and his plays and sonnets are still widely read and performed today

---

The Oxford English Dictionary is the broadest dictionary of the English language. It contains over 600,000 words

The English language has many dialects and variations, with varying accents and slang in different regions of the country

---

The Queen's English is a term used to describe the standard British accent used by the royal family and other upper-class Britons

---

The Cockney accent, which is associated with the East End of London, is known for its distinct pronunciation and slang

The Scottish accent is known for its distinct sound and variations in pronunciation depending on the region

The Welsh language, known as Cymraeg, is an official language in Wales and is spoken by approximately 20% of the population

Irish Gaelic is a Celtic language spoken in parts of Northern Ireland and the Republic of Ireland. It is one of the official languages of the Republic of Ireland

Scots is the form of English spoken in Scotland. It is part of the West Germanic language family

---

The United Kingdom has a rich tradition of poetry, with famous poets including William Wordsworth, John Keats, and T.S. Eliot

---

The UK has a thriving literary scene. It has produced many famous authors such as J.K. Rowling, Charles Dickens, and Jane Austen

Many famous English language novels have been adapted into successful films, such as Harry Potter, Lord of the Rings, and Bridget Jones's Diary

---

The United Kingdom has a rich tradition of storytelling, with famous works such as Beowulf and the Canterbury Tales

---

The term "slang" is believed to have originated in the United Kingdom in the 18th century

The British Library, located in London, is one of the largest libraries in the world and holds over 170 million items

---

The King James Bible, published in 1611, is one of the most famous English language translations of the Bible

---

The English language is one of the most widely spoken languages in the world, spoken by approximately 1.5 billion people worldwide

The UK has a rich tradition of folk music. Many famous musicians such as Bob Dylan and Simon Garfunkel have drawn inspiration from British folk music

---

The United Kingdom has a rich tradition of theatre, with famous playwrights such as Oscar Wilde, and Harold Pinter

---

Many English language words have multiple meanings, making it a complex and nuanced language

The United Kingdom has a long history of linguistic diversity, with languages such as Cornish and Manx now considered endangered

The English language has been heavily influenced by other languages, such as Latin and French, which were spoken by the ruling classes at various points in history

The United Kingdom has produced many famous actors and actresses, who have helped to spread the English language around the world through film and television

The United Kingdom has a long tradition of oral storytelling, with folk tales and legends being passed down through generations

Many famous English language plays have been adapted into successful films, such as My Fair Lady and West Side Story

About 60% of UK's population are Christians

UK's Currency is the British Pound. 1 British Pound (GBP) = 100 pennies

---

The National Anthem of the UK is 'God Save the King'

The National Symbols are the Lion (national animal), Union Jack (national flag) and blue, white and red are the national colours

The first political union of the Kingdom of England which then included Wales and Scotland was formed in 1707. Northern Ireland joined this Union in 1922

The city of London was the largest city in the world from 1835 until 1925

The UK was a member of the European Union, but voted to leave in a referendum in 2016. The process of leaving was called Brexit (British Exit) and was completed on 31st January 2020

No location in the UK is further away from the sea than 125 km/ 77 miles

---

The UK has only one land border, which it forms with Ireland

The UK lies on the prime meridian which marks the Greenwich meridian time zone (GMT)

The UK has 13 British territories that are overseas. Some of them are Cayman Islands
and British Virgin Islands in the Caribbean, Gibraltar on the Iberian Peninsula and Saint Helena in the South Atlantic Ocean

---

The largest country of the United Kingdom is England. The smallest country is Northern Ireland

---

The UK has the third longest coastline in Europe with 12,430 km/ 7,723 miles. Norway
and Denmark (Greenland) come first and second

The highest mountain in the UK is Ben Nevis, Scotland which is 1,345 m/4,412 ft. tall

The largest lake in the UK is Lough Neagh. It is found in Northern Ireland

Loch Ness is the largest fresh water lake, by volume, in the UK

River Severn is the longest river in the UK. It is 354 km/ 220 miles long

London Heathrow is the largest airport in Europe

The Shard skyscraper in London is the tallest building in Europe. It is 310 m/ 1,015 ft. in height

Edinburgh has been the capital city of Scotland since 1437. It is known for its castle and the Royal mile. The International Fringe Festival in the city attracts more than 250,000 visitors every year

---

Windsor is known for its castle, which is a royal residence built in the 11th century.
Windsor castle is the largest inhabited castle in the world

Stonehenge is known as the oldest monument in the world dating back over 3,000
years. These huge rocks are older than the Pyramids

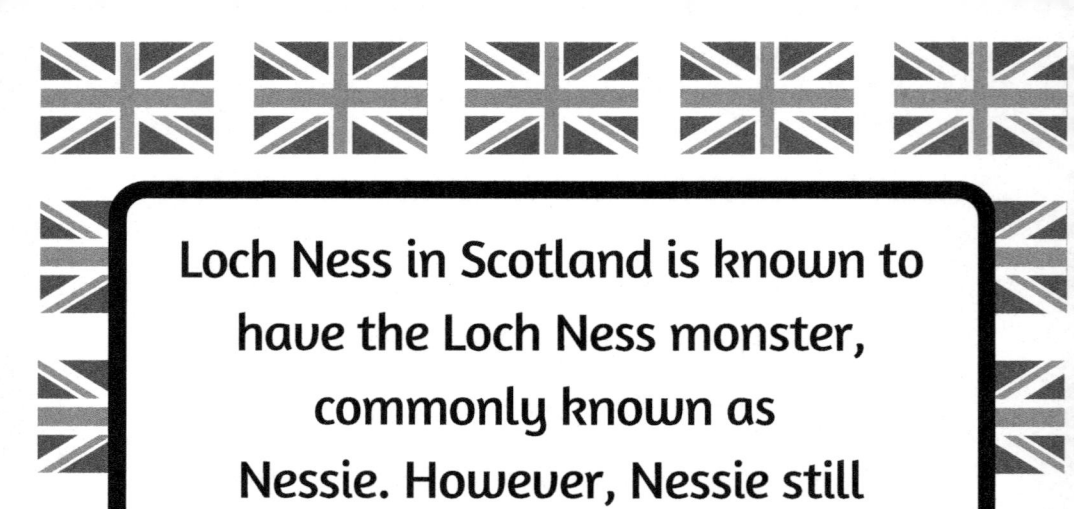

Loch Ness in Scotland is known to have the Loch Ness monster, commonly known as Nessie. However, Nessie still remains a mythical mystery

Cardiff, the capital city of Wales is often referred to as the 'City of Arcades'. It has the most indoor shopping centres in the UK

Belfast is Northern Ireland's main business centre. It is located on the banks of the Lagan River. The city has one of the biggest ports of the UK

Shipbuilding was a major sector for Belfast in the last century. Belfast once had the
biggest shipyard in the world where the RMS Titanic was built in 1912

Florence Nightingale (1820 - 1910) opened the first school for professional nursing in
1860 and helped spread medical knowledge. She was nicknamed the 'lady with a lamp'

J.K. Rowling is the author of 'Harry Potter' book series. She became the first author to earn one billion US dollars in her career as a writer. The seven fantasy novels tell us about the adventures of the young wizard Harry Potter and his friends

The main language spoken in the UK is British English

Scots, Welsh and Irish are also languages spoken in the UK

There are also four Celtic languages spoken. They are Scottish Gaelic, Irish Gaelic, Welch and Cornish

The ancient languages Scottish Gaelic, Irish Gaelic, Welsh and Breton are still spoken in England but only by groups of people

---

French was actually the official language in the UK for about three hundred years, from 1066 - 1362

The Breton language is nowadays mostly spoken by the people in Brittany in north-western France

The United Kingdom is famous for its traditional cuisine, such as fish and chips, roast beef, and bangers and mash

The English breakfast is a famous meal that typically includes eggs, bacon, sausage, black pudding, beans, and toast

The Scotch egg is a hard-boiled egg wrapped in sausage meat and breadcrumbs, and then deep-fried

The Cornish pasty is a savoury pastry filled with meat, potatoes, and vegetables, and is a popular snack in Cornwall

Marmite is a popular spread made from yeast extract. It is often enjoyed on toast or in sandwiches

Battenberg cake is a pink and yellow checkerboard sponge cake that is popular for afternoon tea

Sticky toffee pudding is a dessert made from a sponge cake that is topped with a sticky toffee sauce

---

Blackcurrant squash is a popular drink in the United Kingdom. It is often enjoyed as a refreshing summer drink

---

The Full Scottish Breakfast includes black pudding, haggis, and tattie scones, in addition to other breakfast items

Crumpets are a popular breakfast item in the United Kingdom, and are often served with butter and jam

---

Spotted Dick is a traditional dessert made from suet pastry and dried fruit. It is mostly served with custard

---

Scones are a traditional British teatime treat, and are typically served with jam and clotted cream

Bubble and squeak is a dish made from leftover vegetables. It is served as a breakfast item

Shepherd's pie is a savoury pie made with minced lamb or beef and topped with mashed potatoes

Lemon drizzle cake is a popular dessert in the United Kingdom. It is made with lemon zest and juice

Eccles cakes are a type of pastry filled with currants. They are often enjoyed with a cup of tea

---

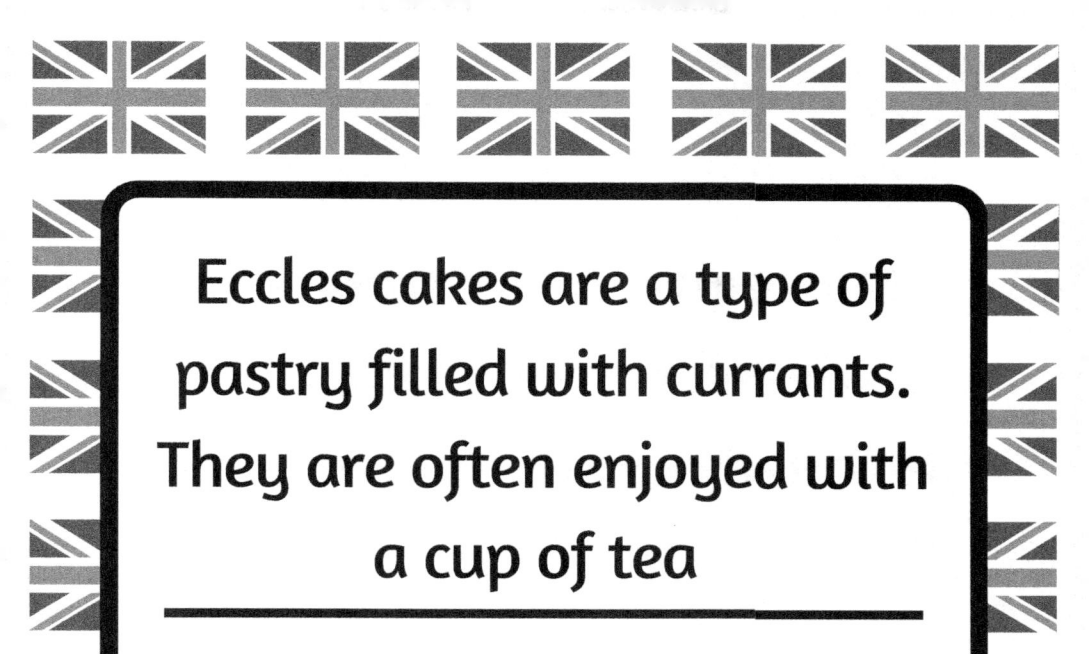

Haggis is a traditional Scottish dish made from sheep's offal, oats, and spices

---

Cider is a popular alcoholic drink in the United Kingdom made from apples or pears

Mince pies are a traditional dessert that is typically enjoyed during the Christmas season

Welsh rarebit is a dish made from melted cheese and other ingredients, and is served on toast

Toad in the hole is a traditional dish made from sausages and Yorkshire pudding batter

Yorkshire pudding is a traditional dish made of batter and typically served with roast beef and gravy

---

Jaffa cakes are a popular snack in the United Kingdom made from sponge cake, orange jelly, and chocolate

---

Steak and kidney pie is a traditional savoury pie made with steak and kidney filling

Hot cross buns are a type of sweet bread that are typically enjoyed during the Easter season

---

Pimm's is a popular alcoholic drink in the United Kingdom served with lemonade and fruit

---

Victoria sponge cake is a popular dessert in the United Kingdom made from sponge cake and jam

Fish cakes are a popular snack in the United Kingdom, and are typically made from mashed potatoes and fish

Gingerbread is a traditional dessert that is often served during the Christmas season

Marmalade is a popular preserve made from oranges or other citrus fruits, and is spread on toast

Cullen skink is a soup made from smoked haddock, potatoes, and onions. It is a traditional Scottish dish

---

Black Pudding is a meal of sausage or sliced meatloaf of pig's blood and fat that has been mixed with pepper or spices and cooked or fried

---

Baked Beans on Toast is a dish made up of baked beans in tomato sauce and is especially popular among children

Afternoon tea is actually a light meal of tea and sandwiches or toast, scones or pastry served in between lunch and dinner. Afternoon tea is taken around 4pm - 5pm in many families when children come home from school.

High tea is a meal eaten in the late afternoon or early evening, typically consisting of a cooked dish, bread and butter, and tea

---

There are over 170 universities in the UK. Six of them are in the world's top 30 universities

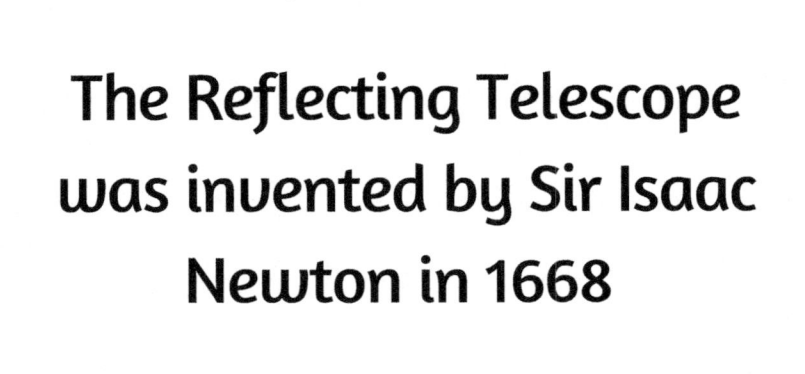

The Reflecting Telescope was invented by Sir Isaac Newton in 1668

The first practical patent for an atmospheric pressure steam engine was filed by Thomas Savery in 1698

Peter Durand is credited with the invention of the tin can in 1810

One of the lesser-known greatest British inventions is the Dewar Flask, vacuum flask or Thermos Flask. Sir James Dewar invented the first vacuum flask in 1892.

Henry Bessemer patented his technique for mass producing steel from molten pig iron in 1856

After Charles Wheatstone and William Cooke successfully built their five-needle system in 1837, instant communication using electricity suddenly became a realit

The yum yum chocolate bars we eat were invented in the UK too! They were first made by JS Fry and Sons in 1847

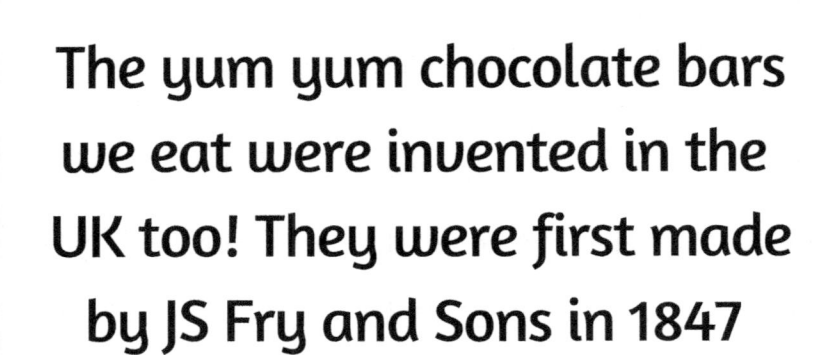

The first fire extinguisher ever patented was in 1723 by Ambrose Godfrey. The modern fire extinguisher was invented by British Captain William Manby in 1818

The world's first ATM was installed at a Barclays Bank in Enfield Town, London in 1967. This was the product of John Shepard-Baron and his team of engineer

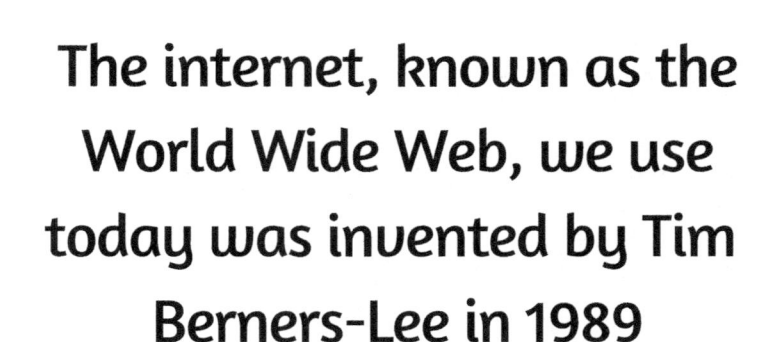

The internet, known as the World Wide Web, we use today was invented by Tim Berners-Lee in 1989

The world's first lawnmower was developed by Edwin Budding in 1830

Thanks to the innovative work of Richard Trevithick in 1804, George Stephenson was able to open the first public railway in 1825. It ran between Stockton and Darlington in England

The world's first automatic kettle was developed by Russel Hobbs in 1955.

Carbonated water, or Soda water, was first invented by Joseph Priestly in 1767.
Remember to thank him whenever you crack open that can of sod

---

Music listened to in the UK include folk music, jazz, rapping/hip hop, pop and rock music

London had the first Hard Rock Café in the world. It opened on June 14, 1971

The word 'sport' was first seen in English in the 15th century. It was a shortened form
of the word 'disport', meaning a diversion from serious duties

---

The French, Italians, Germans, Swedes, Dutch and Danes all adopted the word 'sport'
from the English in the 19th century

In the 1908 Olympics, teams from UK police forces won all the medals in the tug-of-war event

In 1969, David Attenborough wanted to take advantage of colour televisions and a new TV show was introduced called Pot Black which was a snooker tournament programme

Hockey and Polo are the only sport where left-handed play is banned

The first sport to allow women to play alongside men was Croquet

---

The oldest current football anthem is Norwich City's 'On the Ball, City', penned in the 1890's

---

Wimbledon lawn Tennis Association provides free tea for life to competitors who reach the quarter-finals or beyond

Tennis attracts the third largest portion of British gambling money. The number one slot goes to football and number two to racing

---

Manchester United is the most successful football club in the UK. They have won 20 English league titles, 12 FA Cups, and 3 European Cup

---

The most successful tennis player from the UK is Fred Perry. He won eight Grand Slam titles in the 1930s

The Six Nations is an annual rugby union tournament played between England, Scotland, Wales, Ireland, France, and Italy

---

The Boat Race is an annual rowing race between the universities of Oxford and Cambridge. It was first held in 1829

Sir Chris Hoy is the most successful Olympian from the UK. He was a cyclist who won six gold medals

The Commonwealth Games is a multi-sport event held every four years, featuring athletes from countries in the Commonwealth of Nations

Cricket was invented in England in the 16th century and is now played worldwide

The first ever official football match was played in 1863 in London between two teams, one of which later became known as Arsenal

The oldest tennis tournament in the world, Wimbledon, was first held in 1877 and is still held annually in London

---

The Highland Games originated from Scotland. They feature events such as caber tossing, hammer throwing, and tug-of-war

---

Horse racing is a popular sport in the UK. The prestigious Royal Ascot has been held every year since 1711

Rugby originated in England in the 19th century and is now played worldwide,
including the popular Six Nations tournament

The London Marathon is one of the world's most popular and iconic marathons. It was first held in 1981

Snooker is a cue sport popular in the UK. It was invented in India in the 19th century
by British officers stationed there

Darts is a game traditionally played in pubs which originated from the UK in the 19th century. It is now played professionally around the world

---

About 5,000 years ago, much of the United Kingdom was covered with thick forests

---

Roe deer, which are native to the country, and red deer are the largest mammals found in the U.K.

In Wales, one of the most spotted mammals is the red fox

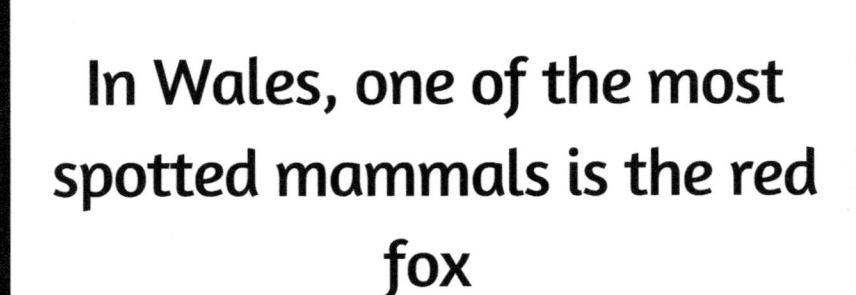

Minke whales, bottlenose dolphins, and orcas can be seen in the waters surrounding the U.K

Oil, iron, and steel products are some of the United Kingdom's main exports, or goods sold to other countries

Over the centuries, the United Kingdom has accumulated wealth from foreign lands the country colonized or took control over

---

In A.D. 43, the Romans invaded England and ruled for nearly 400 years. They built roads, bathhouses, and sewers

---

From the 900s to the 1400s, England was ruled by Viking, Danish, and Norman invaders

In 1485, Welsh noble Henry Tudor claimed the English crown and became Henry VII, the first of five Tudor monarchs

---

The Welsh territory was officially united with England in 1536

Scotland united with England in 1707 after many battles to keep its independence

The union of England, Wales, and Scotland became the kingdom of Great Britain, ruled by Queen Anne. She was the first monarch of the newly-formed Great Britain

---

Ireland officially became united with England, Scotland, and Wales in 1801, forming the United Kingdom of Great Britain and Ireland

---

In 1607, Jamestown, now the state of Virginia, became the first permanent English settlement in the Americas

The UK is known for its beautiful countryside. It has many national parks and areas of outstanding natural beauty such as Peak District National Park

The UK has many famous TV shows and films, such as Doctor Who and Harry Potter

The UK is famous for its pubs, which are a central part of British culture

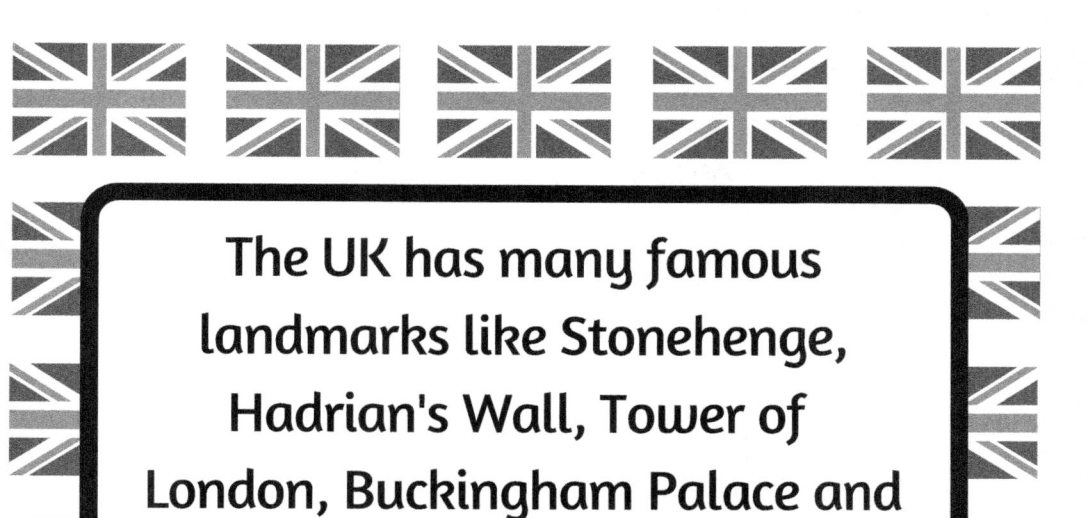

The UK has many famous landmarks like Stonehenge, Hadrian's Wall, Tower of London, Buckingham Palace and Big Ben

The UK is home to many famous museums and art galleries, such as the British Museum and the National Gallery

The UK has a national health service that provides free healthcare to all citizens

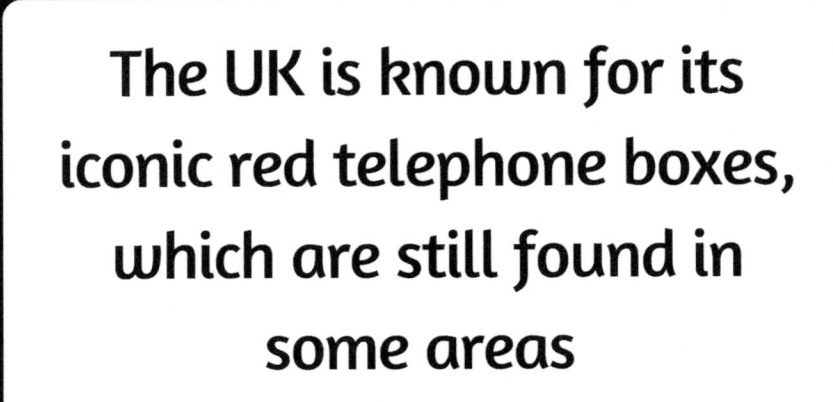

The UK is known for its iconic red telephone boxes, which are still found in some areas

The UK has many famous festivals and celebrations, such as the Notting Hill Carnival and the Edinburgh Fringe Festival

The UK has a rich literary tradition. It has produced many famous authors, poets, and playwrights

The UK is home to many famous universities, such as Oxford and Cambridge

---

The UK has a well-developed transportation system, including trains, buses, and the London Underground

---

The UK has a varied climate. There are milder temperatures in the south and colder temperatures in the north

The UK is known for its love of gardening. Many people cultivate their own gardens

---

The UK has a rich maritime history, with many famous explorers and sailors hailing from the country such as James Cook and Sir Francis Drake

---

The UK has many famous landmarks associated with the Royal Family, such as Windsor Castle and Balmoral

The UK has a long history of music, dating back to the medieval period

---

The Beatles, one of the most famous bands in the world, were from the UK

Other famous British bands include Queen, Pink Floyd, The Rolling Stones, and Oasis

The UK has produced many famous solo artists such as Adele, Ed Sheeran, and Elton John

---

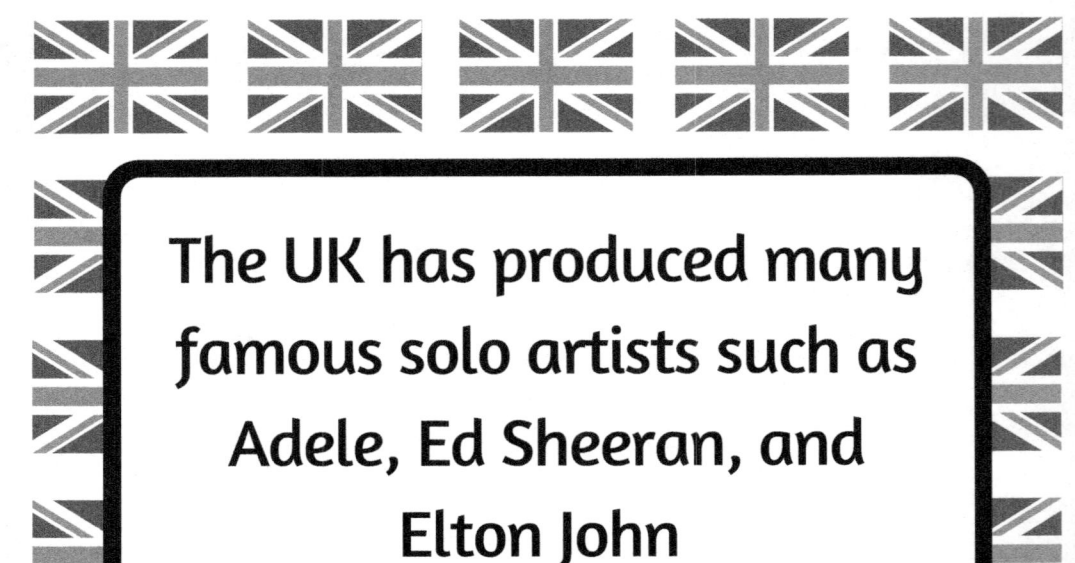

The UK is known for its love of pop music

The UK has a vibrant electronic music scene. It has birthed many famous DJs and producers

The United Kingdom is home to many famous music festivals, such as Glastonbury and Reading & Leeds

The United Kingdom has a rich classical music tradition, with many famous composers such as Benjamin Britten and Edward Elgar

The UK also has a strong choral music tradition. It has many famous choirs like the St. Paul's Cathedral Choir and choral societies

The UK is known for its love of folk music. Many traditional folk songs like Auld Lang Syne are still performed today

---

The first lasting English-language musical was John Gay's The Beggar's Opera in 1728

The UK is known to have a lot of brass bands. Some communities have their own band

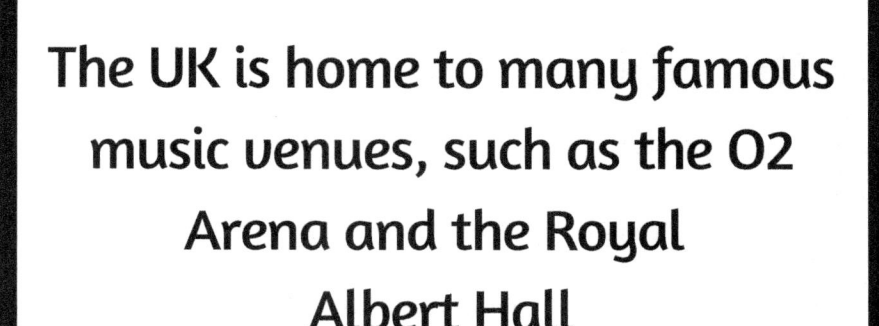

The UK is home to many famous music venues, such as the O2 Arena and the Royal Albert Hall

---

The first computer program was written by Ada Lovelace, a British mathematician, in the mid-19th century

---

The UK is home to many famous technology companies, such as ARM, Imagination Technologies, and Raspberry Pi

The UK is a world leader in the development of artificial intelligence and machine learning

---

The UK has a strong aerospace industry, with many famous companies such as BAE Systems and Rolls-Royce

---

The first passenger railway was built in the UK in the early 19th century

The UK is home to many famous engineering firms, such as Dyson and McLaren

---

The UK is a world leader in the development of renewable energy technologies, such as wind and solar power

---

The United Kingdom is known for its advanced medical research. It has had famous
scientists like Stephen Hawking and Charles Darwin and doctors hailing from the country

The UK has famous universities that specialise in science and technology, such as University of Cambridge and Imperial College London

The UK is a world leader in the development of fintech (financial technology). Many new start-ups have originated from the country

The United Kingdom is known for its love of video games, with many famous game development studios such as Rockstar North and Rare

The UK is a world leader in the development of block chain technology and cryptocurrency

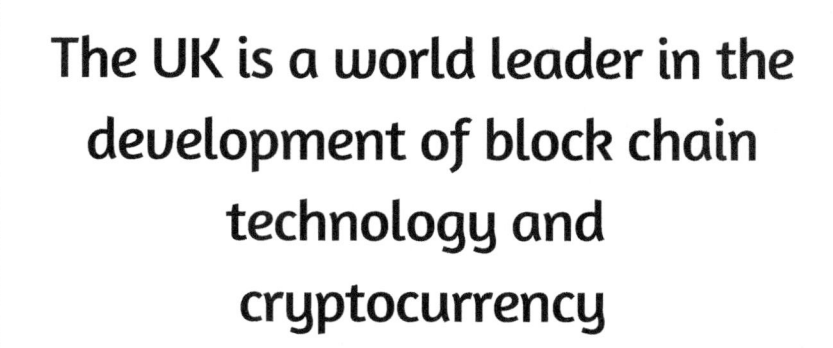

The United Kingdom has many famous museums and exhibitions that showcase technological and scientific innovations, like the Science Museum in London

The United Kingdom was once part of the Roman Empire. Many of the country's ancient buildings and monuments date back to this time

The United Kingdom was a major player in both World War I and World War II. It played a key role in the defeat of Nazi Germany

The UK was the birthplace of the Industrial Revolution. This transformed the country from an agricultural to an industrialised nation

The first UK parliament was established in the 13th century

Famous authors such as Charles Dickens, and Jane Austen were from the United Kingdom

The UK has a long history of artistic and cultural contributions. Banksy and Henry Moore were famous artists from the country

The UK played a key role in the formation of the United Nations and the European Union

Winston Churchill has been widely seen as one of the greatest leaders in British history. He was also a painter and writer

---

Margaret Thatcher was the first female Prime Minister of the United Kingdom

---

Queen Elizabeth II owned more than 30 corgis during her reign

Queen Victoria reigned for 63 years and was the longest-reigning monarch in British history until Queen Elizabeth II surpassed her record

---

Oliver Cromwell was responsible for the execution of King Charles I during the English Civil War

---

William Pitt the Younger became Prime Minister at the age of 24 and was known for his effective leadership during the Napoleonic War

Elizabeth I was known as the Virgin Queen because she never married or had children during her reign

David Lloyd George was the first Welshman to serve as Prime Minister and led the country during World War I

Tony Blair, who served as Prime Minister from 1997 to 2007, was the youngest Prime Minister since William Pitt the Younger

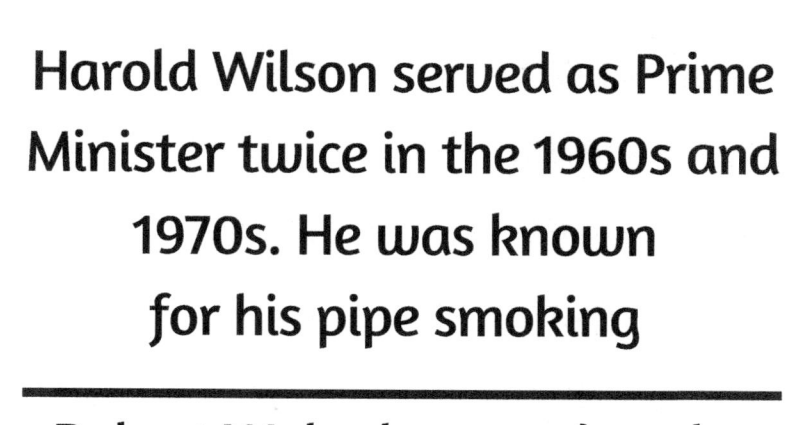

Harold Wilson served as Prime Minister twice in the 1960s and 1970s. He was known for his pipe smoking

Robert Walpole served as the first Prime Minister of Great Britain in the 18th century. He lay the foundation for the modern British political system

Theresa May was the second female Prime Minister of the United Kingdom. She is a keen lover of fashion and has been featured in Vogue magazine

David Cameron, who served as Prime Minister from 2010 to 2016, was related to Queen Elizabeth II through a distant ancestor

---

James Callaghan was the first person to hold the title of Prime Minister without being a member of the House of Lords

---

Tony Blair's wife, Cherie Blair, was the first Prime Minister's spouse to have a career as a barrister

Henry VIII had six wives and was a skilled musician and composer

---

Harold Macmillan served as Prime Minister in the late 1950s and early 1960s. He was also a successful author and historian

---

Winston Churchill was a writer who won the Nobel Prize in Literatures in 1953

The Thatcher effect is named after the then British Prime Minister Margaret Thatcher, on whose photograph the effect was first demonstrated

Queen Elizabeth II was a keen equestrian. She owned and bred many horses over the years.

Queen Victoria was a devoted writer. She kept a detailed journal throughout her reign

Oliver Cromwell was best known for being Lord Protector of the Commonwealth of England Scotland and Ireland after the defeat of King Charles I in the Civil War

---

William Pitt the Younger suffered from poor health throughout his life, and died at the age of 46

Elizabeth I was known for her love of music and the arts. She was a patron of many famous writers and artists

Henry VIII was a talented athlete in his youth. He was known for his skill at jousting

David Lloyd George was known for his radical views and his efforts to reform the British political system

The Ryder Cup is a biennial golf competition between Europe and the United States. The first contest was in 1927

The Ryder Cup has been won by the United Kingdom 17 times, the second most of any country after the United States

---

The oldest football club in the world is Sheffield FC, which was founded in 1857 in Sheffield, England

---

The London 2012 Olympic Games were the most successful ever for the United Kingdom. The country won 29 gold medals and finished third in the medal table

The British Grand Prix is held annually at the Silverstone Circuit in Northamptonshire. It is one of the oldest and most prestigious races in Formula One

---

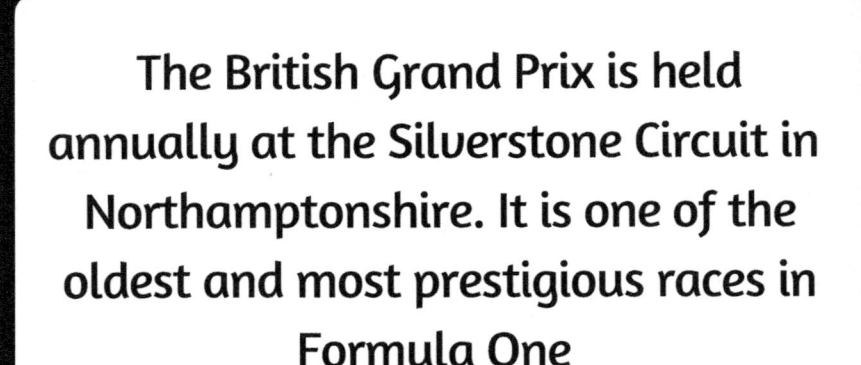

Athletics, including track and field events, is a popular sport in the United Kingdom, with many famous British athletes such as Mo Farah and Jessica Ennis-Hill

---

The Six Nations rugby tournament, contested between England, Wales, Scotland, Ireland, France, and Italy, is one of the most prestigious rugby competitions in the world

The British and Irish Lions, a rugby union team that represents the United Kingdom and Ireland, is famous for its tours of Australia, New Zealand, and South Africa

---

The Oxford-Cambridge Boat Race has been held annually since 1856, with the exception of the two World Wars

---

Horse racing is a popular sport in the United Kingdom. There are many famous races such as the Grand National and the Epsom Derby

The Premier League, the top tier of English football, is one of the most popular sports leagues in the world

---

The Ashes is a biennial cricket competition between England and Australia, and is one of the oldest and most fiercely contested rivalries in sports

---

The first modern Olympic Games were held in Athens, Greece in 1896, but the United Kingdom has hosted the Games three times, in 1908, 1948, and 2012

The London Marathon, held annually in London, is one of the world's most popular long-distance running events

---

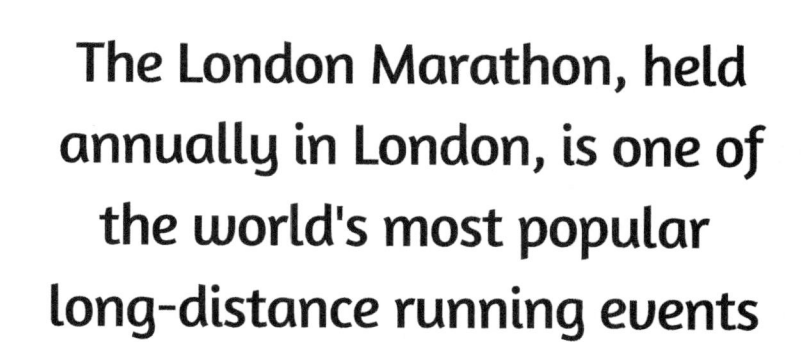

The Scottish Highland Games is a traditional Scottish event featuring athletic competitions such as caber tossing and hammer throwing. It has been held for centuries

---

The first recorded use of the word "sandwich" was in 1762, when the fourth Earl of Sandwich asked for a slice of meat between two slices of bread so he could eat without interrupting his gambling game

The UK is home to more than 700 different types of cheese

The most popular cheese in the UK is cheddar

The first recorded use of the word "chocolate" in English was in 1604

The Football Association (FA), founded in 1863, is the oldest football association in the world

---

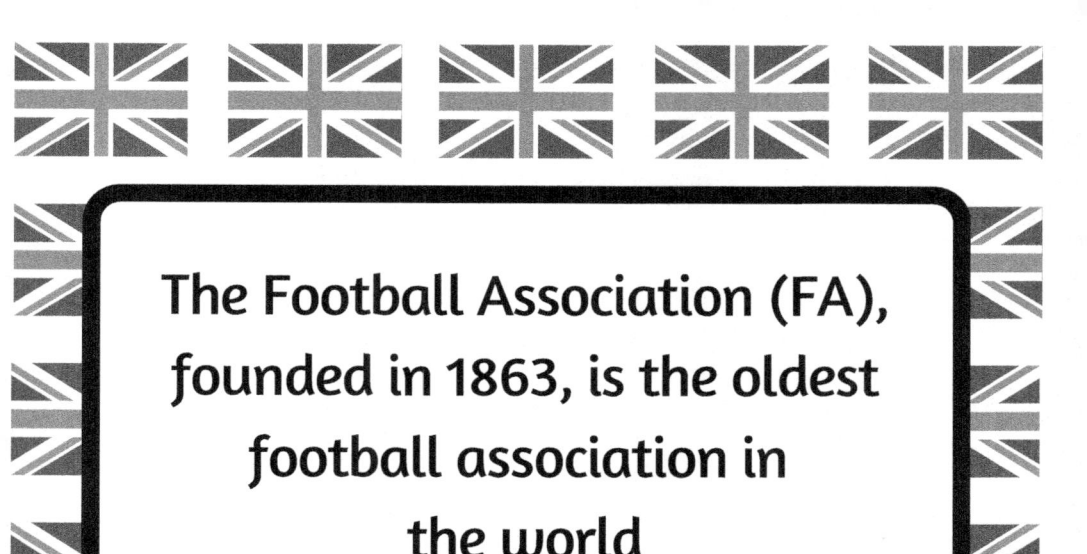

Cadbury's chocolate was founded in Birmingham, UK, in 1824

The first tea shop in the UK opened in 1657 in London

The most popular tea in the UK is black tea, often served with milk and sugar

---

The UK is famous for its beer, with over 1,500 breweries producing more than 14,000 different types of beer

---

The most popular beer in the UK is ale

The UK is the largest producer of gin in the world

Gin was originally used as a medicine to treat stomach problems

---

The most popular gin cocktail in the UK is the gin and tonic

The UK is famous for its whisky, with Scotland being the largest producer

The UK is home to the world-famous Harrods department store, which has a food hall selling some of the finest foods in the world

The UK is known for its love of pies, with the most popular being steak and kidney pie

Bangers and mash is a dish consisting of sausages and mashed potatoes. It is a traditional British meal

---

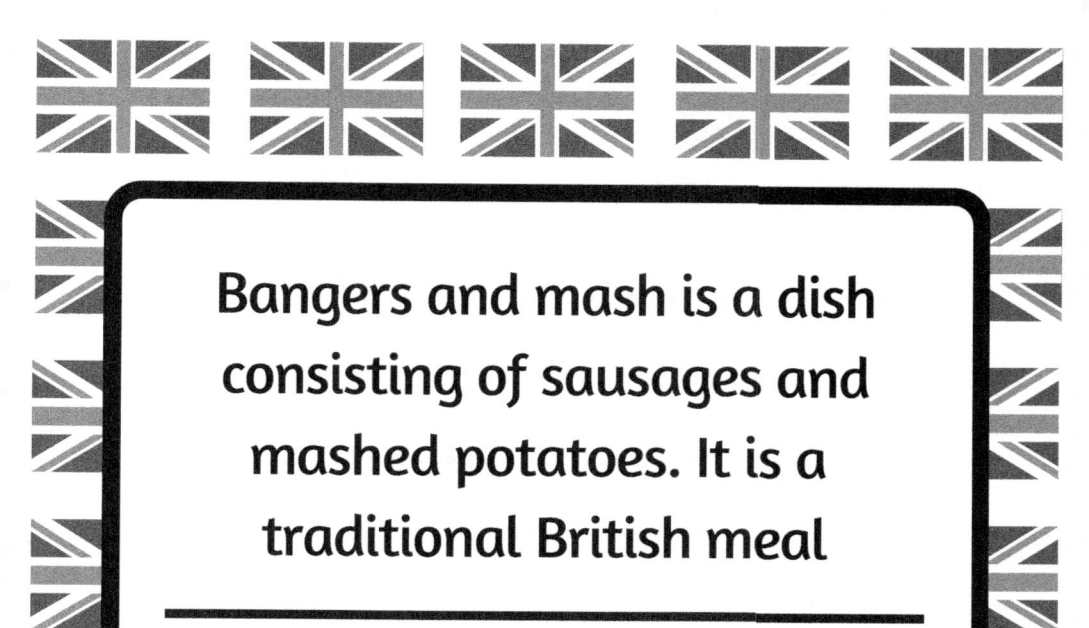

The UK is home to many famous chocolate brands, including Cadbury's, Thornton's, and Lindt

---

The most popular soft drink in the UK is Coca-Cola

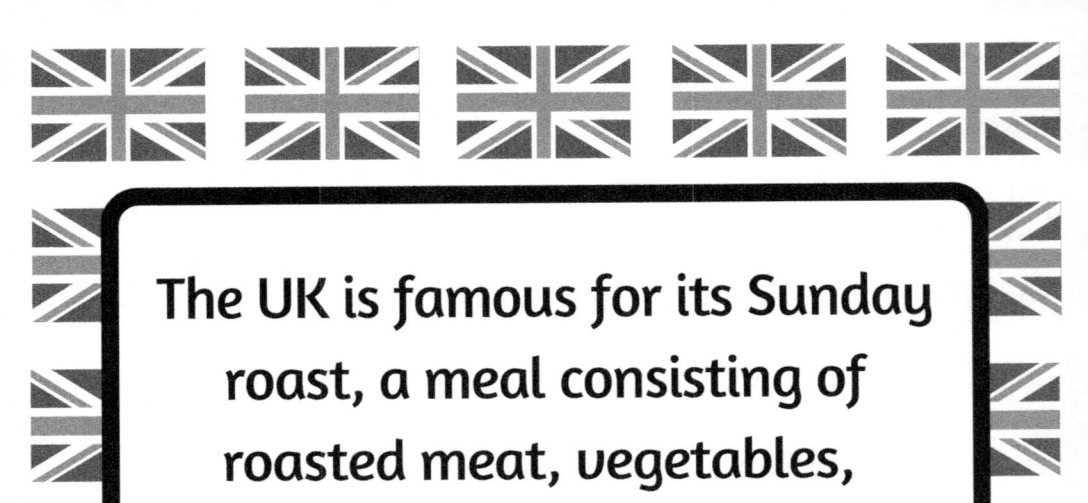

The UK is famous for its Sunday roast, a meal consisting of roasted meat, vegetables, and gravy

The most popular fast food restaurant in the UK is McDonald's

The most popular pizza topping in the UK is pepperoni

The UK is famous for its love of Indian food. There are many Indian restaurants located throughout the country

---

Chicken tikka masala is a popular dish in the UK and is often referred to as the national dish

---

The UK is known for its love of pubs. There are thousands located throughout the country

The most popular pub snack in the UK is the pork scratchings

The UK is home to many famous brands of crisps, including Walkers and Pringles

---

The most popular flavour of crisps in the UK is salt and vinegar

The UK has a diverse population. Significant numbers of immigrants from countries such as India, Pakistan, and the Caribbean can be found in the country

---

The UK has a rich history of musical theatre. Famous musicals including Les Misérables and Phantom of the Opera originated from the UK

Llanfairpwllgwyngyllgogerychwyrndrobwllllantysiliogogogoch is a village
in Anglesey in Wales. It has the longest town name in Europe

You can receive a personalised card from the King on your hundredth birthday. In fact, in the United Kingdom, you can apply for one for your 105th birthday too – and for each birthday year after

---

The King has seven residences in total across the UK, the most famous of which is Buckingham Palace in the centre of London

---

The Chancellor is the only person allowed to in the House of Commons while they deliver the annual Budget speech, which outlines the government's economic policies for the year

The BBC is paid for by the public with an annual TV licensing fee of about £160. This is why they do not show adverts in between programmes

---

Once a year, competitors compete in a cheese rolling competition at Cooper's Hill in Gloucestershire, where they chase a 3.2 kg wheel of double Gloucester cheese down a hill

---

The British pound is the oldest currency in the world that is still being used

If you lay the books in all of the shelves of the British Library at King's Cross end to end, it would be 746 kilometres long and could stretch from London to Aberdeen

---

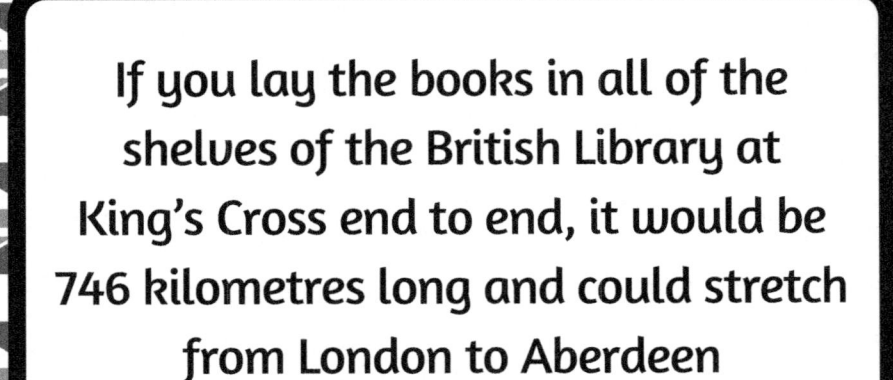

For a short time in the 1700s, the King banned golf because it was interrupting archery and military practice

---

Agatha Christie's The Mousetrap has been running since 1952, which makes it the longest-running show of any kind in the world

The United Kingdom was the first country to use postage stamps

---

Big Ben is actually the name of the bell rather than the clock. The tower has recently undergone renovation, which meant that its bell fell silent for a few years

---

On the grounds of the Tower of London, there must always be at least six ravens at any one time. This is due to an ancient decree put in place by King Charles II. It is said that if this rule is broken, the monarchy will fall

Scan The QR Code To Check Out More Utopia Press Books On Amazon!

© **Copyright 2022 by Utopia Press**

All rights reserved. The content contained within this book may not be reproduced, duplicated or transmitted without direct written permission from the author or the publisher

ISBN: 1095354663

Imprint: Independently published

For any questions or enquiries please email us and we would happily available to help and positive reviews and ratings are greatly appreciated

theutopiapress@gmail.com

Printed in Great Britain
by Amazon